BASKET BOUNTY

JACK KRAMER

BASKET BOUNTY

Growing Vegetables, Fruits, & Herbs
In and Around the House

DRAWINGS BY
Michael Valdez and James Carew

CHARLES SCRIBNER'S SONS
New York, N.Y.

Copyright © 1975 Jack Kramer

Library of Congress Cataloging in Publication Data
Kramer, Jack, 1927-
Basket bounty.
Includes index.
1. Vegetable gardening. 2. Fruit-culture.
3. Herb gardening. I. Title.
SB321.K7   635'.04'8   74-31455
ISBN 0-684-14109-4

This book published simultaneously in the
United States of America and in Canada—
Copyright under the Berne Convention

1 3 5 7 9 11 13 15 17 19 MD/C 20 18 16 14 12 10 8 6 4 2

Printed in the United States of America

ESEATUB -31455

CONTENTS

v

BASKET BOUNTY

HARVEST FOR THE HOME

Years ago in my Chicago apartment I grew chives on a kitchen window-sill and had an orange tree in the dining room. I summered the tree on the back porch; occasionally it would bear a small orange or two. I also had lettuce growing under artificial light. I do not know if it was the taste of these foodstuffs that intrigued me or the satisfaction of coaxing the plants to bear, but I do know that it scotched reports that you can-not grow vegetables and fruits at home. True, the bounty was anything but prodigious, but it opened the door to future growing fun.

Since then I have grown an assortment of herbs, small fruits (peaches are a prime example), and vegetables in and around the house. The difference in taste between a home-grown product and the commercial types has been emphasized enough elsewhere, so I will not labor the point. Your own produce simply tastes better; there is no doubt about it. You will find too that there is a psychological difference in picking your own strawberries, harvesting your own carrots, or snipping herbs for a savory stew. It feels good and is good for you (not to mention the savings involved).

Even if you have little outdoor space (balcony, doorway), you can grow small fruits and vegetables. Today there are many midget vegetables and dwarf fruits that can be grown in the most confined areas. For example, small plum tomatoes are almost infallible, the dwarf peach tree is a sturdy plant that responds well indoors, and of course herbs can be grown easily on a kitchen windowsill.

On a patio two large planter boxes filled with vegetables flank a long planter. Squash, cucumbers, and green peppers revel in sunlight and produce their crops. (Photo by author)

Tomatoes in container at the back door; across the way onions grow in a tub a step away from the kitchen. (Photo by Barr)

THE DELICIOUS VEGETABLES

Growing vegetables is not unlike growing house plants; both need water, good soil, ample light, comfortable temperatures, and humidity. If you are able to grow a pot plant, you can also grow vegetables, fruits, and herbs. The main consideration with bounty growing is space, what the plant grows in, and selection. But do not expect miracles. You will not be able to have corn at the windowsill or watermelons in the dining room, but you can have the delightful midget varieties of tomatoes and carrots. You can grow lettuce, spinach, radishes, and onions or even have tiny cucumbers. There is an amazing array of small vegetables to grow at home; suppliers' catalogs (listed in back of the book) will provide hints and encouragement to get you started.

Most vegetables need some sun; others, like carrots, beets, and spinach, do fine in bright light. All need copious watering. If you are not

Tiny tomatoes only 45 days from planting are ready for harvesting. These are in a handsome pot on the patio. (Photo by Stokes Seeds Co.)

prepared to furnish these essentials, buy your produce at the market and forget about the whole idea.

You can start most vegetables from seed early in the season indoors, say, March or April, to get a head start on spring and then put them in containers outdoors when weather is warm and frosts are over. Or you can buy prestarted plants—lettuce, chard, tomatoes, cucumbers—at your local nursery in seasonal times. Then just plant. (See Chapter 4.)

Some vegetables are known as warm-season crops. That is, they are started in early spring, generally indoors, or outdoors when danger of

A dwarf orange tree graces this table; in summer it is put on a porch to bloom and bear fruit; thus it is both a decorative plant and an eating one. (Photo by Hort Pix)

frost is over; this includes beans, cucumbers, squash, peppers, tomatoes. They thrive in hot weather. Other vegetables, like beets, chard, cauliflower, and cabbage, are cool-season growers, meaning they can take cool weather. Crops like lettuce, radishes, and carrots can be started almost any time to yield successfully through spring to early fall, depending upon the variety.

Strawberries fill this box and in summer bear profusely. Walk to the patio or deck and pick your breakfast fruit. (Photo by author)

① Select materials

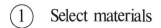

② Measure vertical and horizontal posts, nail together

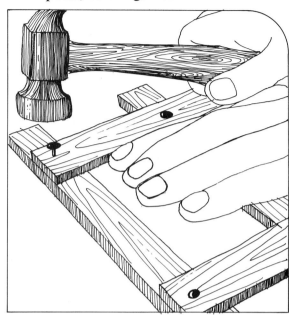

③ Carefully secure posts into soil

④ Attach stems to trellis with string for support

How to Make a Trellis for Climbing Vegetables

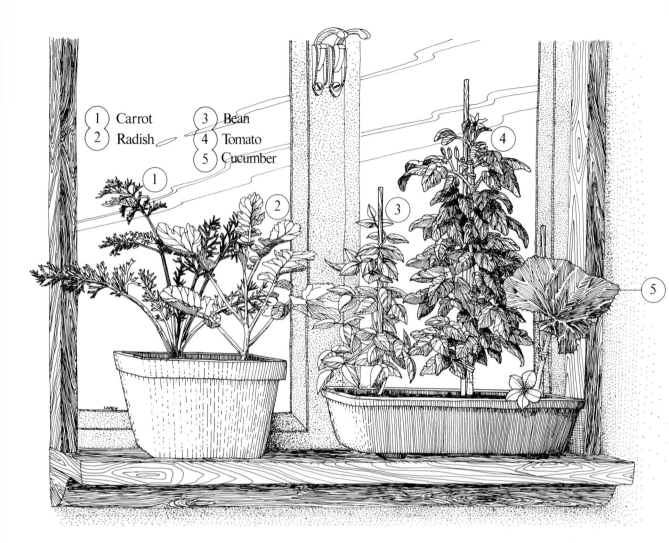

1. Carrot
2. Radish
3. Bean
4. Tomato
5. Cucumber

A Vegetable Window Garden

LUSCIOUS FRUITS

The orange tree I had years ago was a mature, standard-sized tree that eventually touched the 11-foot ceiling in the room. Now there are dwarf trees no bigger than 3 feet that will bear large fruits (the Bonanza Peach immediately comes to mind), as well as lemons and limes, grapefruits, and even loquats and mangoes if you want to get very exotic. Small citrus and peach trees are available at nurseries. It is senseless to try and start your own citrus seed, unless you just want some fun. However, you will have to start exotic fruits like papayas from seed—a tricky but fascinating procedure briefly explained in Chapter 8. Exotic fruits require very special conditions and considerations, but they are a challenge for the adventurous.

It is all a matter of selection, good care, and common sense if you want these luscious fruits on your table a few minutes after picking them. Hybridizers have done an incredible job in supplying us with an assortment of fruits. Louis XIV of France had to grow oranges in silver tubs in specially built glass structures, but you can have fruit-producing trees in and around the house for less money and still live like a king.

Once you start and pick your first home-grown fruit, you will probably think you can grow anything, even bananas, because you will have such a feeling of exaltation. But you cannot. There are limitations, so it is wise to start with a humble approach and a few fruits. Experiment later after you have once reaped some harvest.

SAVORY HERBS

It has taken the public years to discover the joy of snipping their home-grown herbs for cooking. All kinds of herb kitchen gardens are possible. Herbs even come in preplanted kits. Theoretically all you do is punch the plastic envelope, open it, add water, put the plant on a windowsill, and get ready for harvest. Alas, it is not quite that easy; you must be an excellent gardener to get kit herbs really going. I prefer to start my own seeds and take it from there. Also, it is much cheaper. Herbs may be used, and beautifully too, simply for scent or for medicinal purposes.

Dill, savory, and borage are three excellent annual herbs that germinate quickly. Parsley is another quickie that grows without too much encouragement, and chives and oregano are still other easy possibilities. Basil is a must for flavoring tomato dishes.

Most herbs need only good sunlight to grow; containers may be almost anything, and soil can be quite bad, so there is no reason why you should not have them. What is important, I think, is when to pick them and how to dry and store them properly; we shall look into these matters in Chapter 9.

Vegetables, fruits, and herbs offer many enjoyments, and not only in the eating. There is great satisfaction in growing your own, great joy in harvesting the produce, and equal pleasure in eating it. And there is something else: the reward of living, growing things near you —a psychological plus of which you may not even be aware.

Basil is easy to grow and does well in a planter box; this is a good herb with many excellent uses. (Photo by author)

THE HOME GROWING AREA

People who grow plants indoors balk and say it is impossible to grow edible delights. Let me mention again that the house plant, the vegetable, the small fruit tree, or the herb have just the same requirements as a house plant: a bright or sunny place, a good soil, water, and a suitable container. What it really boils down to is where to put plants and what to grow them in. Then tender loving but not smothering care is needed. Once you decide where you want the plants and what they are going to be grown in, you are halfway home.

WHERE TO PUT PLANTS

A bright, sunny place is the best place for most plants. This means somewhere near a window, and quite frankly that is the way it has to be unless you use artificial light. The more light you can give a plant the better it will grow. If natural light is scarce in your apartment or house, do not give up; there may be areas of light you never thought about. How about that little balcony or doorway area? What about that neglected place on the porch? How about the roof (this area can be an excellent vegetable garden, and I have seen many in Chicago and New York) or perhaps even a homemade window greenhouse, small but very useful?

The Balcony Garden

Many high-rise buildings and condominiums have small balconies. These are ideal places for trellises, against which you can grow climbing vegetables such as squash, or cucumbers, with a few pots of herbs at ground level. Just remember that with the balcony garden you should limit yourself to a few things rather than create a jungle which takes over the space.

Also, much as you may be tempted, do not set pots on ledges where they can be accidentally knocked over. A pot filled with soil falling from any height is a hazardous thing. Keep containers at floor level, or, as mentioned, use trellises. Set wooden planters, rectangular or square (easily made), or store-bought window boxes on the floor. Insert wooden stakes or trellises (sold at nurseries), and start your small garden.

Because many balconies are quite windy, make sure plants and pots are well anchored. With a lot of wind, plants dry out quickly, so always keep the watering can handy. To avoid intense noon sun that can harm plants, use suitable sun screens.

Left: *Pots of vegetables such as this can be grown on a balcony where there is good light.* (Photo by author)

Right: *Green peppers and squash share a box on a patio; these are nice leafy vegetables and add beauty to the area.* (Photo by author)

Right: *Leafy lettuce is part of this backyard garden; it looks good and is better to eat.* (Photo by Stokes Seeds Co.)

Left: *A backyard garden full of good eating; the area is only 10 x 20 feet.* (Photo by J. Wilson)

The Patio Garden

Patios and terraces are more for entertaining than for growing plants, but there is no reason for not doing both. And container gardening with vegetables is an excellent way of decorating the patio area. Boxes can be built to fit specific areas; a handsome stair-step arrangement is a good way of conserving space.

On a sunny patio you can grow all kinds of vegetables and herbs and garden to your heart's content. The main things, again, are suitable containers for plants; these are discussed later in this chapter.

The Doorway Garden

Even if your garden area is limited to a doorway area, you can grow some vegetables and herbs. A well-considered use of a few plants can make these tiny areas welcome spots and provide foodstuffs. Consider a tub filled with an assortment of herbs, or perhaps a few containers of tiny tomatoes or midget cucumbers. Do not try to grow anything large or overbearing in these areas; select the small and pretty plants.

Never crowd the area with so many pots that they impede traffic. Instead, use a few well-chosen containers placed to one side of the doorway, or if there are steps at one edge, leave space for foot traffic. Again, do not try to grow corn or massive plants; stick to the small varieties mentioned in Chapter 7.

The Backyard Garden

It is quite amazing what you can do with the smallest piece of land. The first inclination of the home owner is for an ornamental garden with trees and shrubs, but in small places this may be totally out of scale. A neat but compact vegetable garden may be more in keeping with the total landscape plan, and will lessen the burden on your pocketbook. You do not need an elaborate plan, just a simple bed of soil confined in a planter where you can grow some vegetables. Carrots, beets, spinach, and lettuce are all good possibilities, if light is not too good. Where there is ample sun, you can grow practically any kind of crop.

The planter bed is a much neater arrangement than growing plants directly in the soil because you can dictate size and also furnish the proper soil rather than working with or revitalizing what is already there. Use good rich soil, and start plants accordingly, depending upon climate. Use cool- or warm-season vegetables, depending upon your individual site.

You can start plants indoors and move them outdoors when frost is over, or, weather permitting, sow seed directly in beds outdoors. Keep plants well watered and feed regularly. (See Chapter 6 for more information about backyard gardening.)

The Rooftop Garden

A rooftop garden is a treasure. It is a fine retreat from busy day activities and a good place to grow vegetables because there is ample sun. Even the smallest rooftop can accommodate some planter beds of vegetables in pots, or tubs, if you prefer. Wind can be a hazard, but there are ways to combat this; they are discussed in Chapter 5.

Even bushel baskets can be used for vegetables; gold beans such as these have a heavy harvest. (Photo courtesy Stokes Seeds Co.)

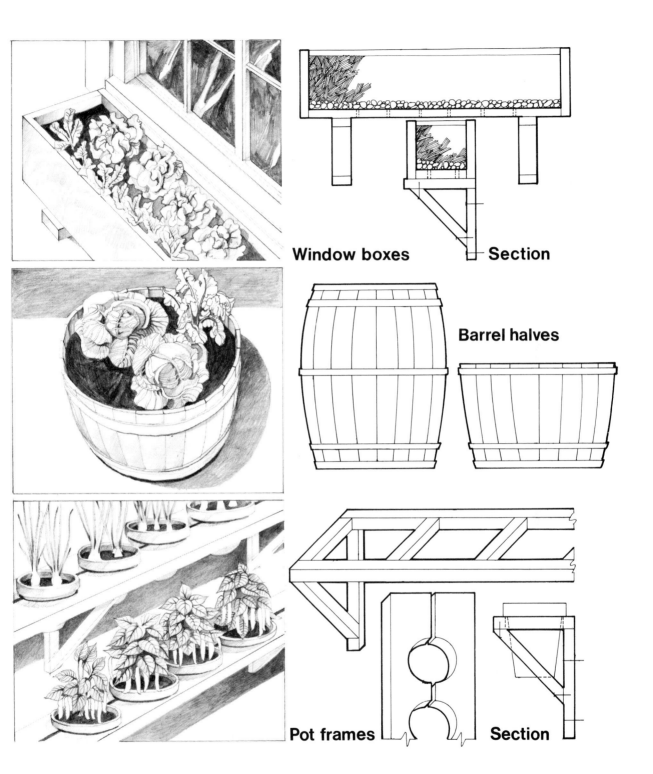

Window boxes   Section

Barrel halves

Pot frames   Section

Vegetable Containers

There is a wide assortment of containers for vegetables, herbs and fruit trees at suppliers. Note the strawberry jars. (Photo by author)

Window Greenhouses

These structures are quite popular because they can be attached to a window with little trouble and provide a nice green effect. However, you *cannot* grow mature vegetables in these areas. Generally the window greenhouse is about 36 x 60 inches, which is fine for starting some vegetables in seed pans or growing some house plants, but for even a modicum of farming you will have to use other areas. However, for getting seeds started the window greenhouse is perfectly satisfactory.

WHAT TO PUT PLANTS IN: CONTAINERS

At one time the clay pot was considered the only logical container for a plant. Today we know better; there are hundreds of containers, mainly the commercial types sold at nurseries and garden shops. Do not overlook making your own containers. These can be really great when you make them to fit specific areas, and they look good if you are a halfway decent carpenter. Even if they do not look good they are unique—one of a kind—because you made them. And putting containers together is not that much work.

It may seem that I attacked the standard clay pot in the first paragraph. Not so. I still think it is an excellent housing for a plant. Water evaporates from the pot slowly; it is a durable, inexpensive pot and now comes in all sizes, from 2 to 24 inches, with variations in design, from a Venetian style to a perfect cylinder. Depths vary, diameters vary, and designs vary, so select something that pleases you and fits the space.

Wooden tubs and planters like wine barrels cut in half and steel-banded soy tubs are good containers and available at modest prices, or there are very fine ornamental tubs that will cost you ten times as much as the plant they contain. Do consider such household containers as coffee cans, ice cream cartons, plastic bleach containers, small garbage cans, barrels, and bushel baskets. There are also plastic and styrofoam containers, hanging baskets (for lettuce, for example), and on and on.

GROWING IS KNOWING

You can—and many people do—grow plants without knowing much about their needs and requirements, but eventually you will want to (and have to) know just how to care for your plants so they prosper. A little bit of knowledge can save you time and trouble, and there is really no hocus-pocus about it. Growing your own vegetables, herbs, and fruits successfully depends upon good soil, proper light and air, watering and feeding, humidity, and plant protection.

You should strive for a perfect balance of each of these cultural aspects, but because few people are perfect, mistakes will be made. However, plants are adaptable and will survive if you remember to water and feed them occasionally.

SOIL

Plants, especially vegetables, need a good balanced nutritional soil. Without it they will not grow or bear their harvest. Although house plants can get along with a less rich soil and still grow, vegetables will

21

not. So unless you want only an ornamental cabbage for your window-sill, supply plants with the best soil. Remember that anything to be eaten must be grown quickly and lushly. Herb plants are exceptions, but vegetables need rapid, unchecked growth.

Like all things today, soil comes in many different guises: in packages, by the bushel, by the truckload, from the yard, and so on. In addition, there are all kinds of soil: Some is screened of rocks and debris, some has added compost, and some has added fertilizers. Thus, when you choose soil you are selecting more than just dirt.

Some gardeners prefer to mix their own soil; that is, they add loam and sand and this and that to make a healthy, friable mix. This is the

Good soil is crumbly and porous with organic matter in it; air and water pass easily through soil like this to assure good crop growth. (Photo USDA)

most satisfactory approach as there is no way of knowing what is in a packaged soil or a bushel of soil bought from the local dealer. However, for the city dweller, hauling tons of soil into the apartment becomes a chore and may even be impossible, so it is the satisfactory packaged soils that will be preferred.

A Suitable Growing Medium

A seed packet or any garden book will invariably tell you to put plants in a rich, friable soil. Just what is a rich, friable soil? Rich means a soil that is high in organic content or soil micro-organisms that transform chemical matter into food for the plant. Friable may be a misleading word, so let us use instead the phrase, a soil that has good air circulation. Air must get into soil to carry water. Root crops such as carrots, which bear into the soil, cannot do so if soil is clay and hard. A carrot that has to struggle to penetrate soil develops more fiber; the more fiber, the less sugar.

For vegetables you will need a soil that has some compost because compost (decayed organic matter) increases the friability of the soil. It actually loosens soil structure. It is out of the question for the average apartment dweller or even small home owner to have a mountain of compost in the backyard, so buy composts or manure in tidy sacks at nurseries.

Nitrogen is absolutely necessary for plants to grow, and even though the packaged soil you may buy has some, you should add more. Bone meal, blood meal, and cottonseed meal all have high percentages of nitrogen and are sold in sacks at nurseries. Again, the idea is to furnish a really rich soil that will bring vegetables to their best in a short time.

Packaged Mixes

Some people argue that a packaged mix used for plant growth is like a packaged cake, but I have found that packaged cake mixes, when given proper additives such as an extra egg and milk instead of water, produce a fairly good cake. So it is with packaged soil mixes. Add to it by using the ingredients mentioned above. How much? A handful of this, a handful of that? Specific directions are in the next section. The problem with packaged mixes is that there are too many; some are for African violets only, others for begonias, some for seed starting, some for cactus, others for God knows what. Since the soil is packaged it is impossible to know just what is in it, and because there are no markings on the package, how do you tell without opening a package? Generally I feel and squeeze. This is hardly a scientific method, but it is the only way. If the packaged soil is loose, gives in my hand, and is fairly dark in color, I hope that is what I need. If the package feels hard and grainy in my hand, I look further.

Although bushels of soil bought at the local nursery are not packaged soils per se, they are included here because you can see and feel what you buy, and guesswork is eliminated. Bushel soil is cheaper than packaged stuff. Run your hand through the soil; it should feel like a mealy, well-done baked potato. Also study the color; it should be rich brown. Essentially, when you buy soil by the bushel from a nursery or greenhouse you are getting the same soil they use. It will contain all necessary ingredients and normally produce very good plant growth.

Soil-less Mixes

In addition to the normal packaged mixes, dealers also carry soil-less mixes. These are fine for some vegetables because they eliminate the danger of root nematode and some soil-borne diseases. Indeed, tomatoes and peppers do excellently in soil-less mixes, from all reports I have had. But being a purist, I like soil—the smell and feel of it—and use it for vegetables. However, if you want to try the soil-less mixes—and they are lightweight too—go ahead. But remember that you will have to give plants regular feeding when they are grown in such mixes.

Soil You Mix

If you are frugal, you can mix your own soil by taking dirt from your yard or wherever (for example, from a friend's yard) and using it. This involves a hazard because soils should be sterile, that is, not have any fungus disease carried in the spores of soil which can cause a multitude of sins, namely, damping off. This disease can quickly ruin a crop of seedlings: Plants will sprout, and then suddenly stems will collapse almost overnight. To avoid damping off and other fungus possibilities, if you take dirt from a yard to use as soil, sterilize it. This is not a very happy experience; it smells! To sterilize soil, bake it in a flat cookie sheet for about 1 hour at 215° with the oven door open. Let the soil stand for a few more days to allow ammonia released in the heating process to escape.

For the perfectionist there is the mix-your-own-soil recipe: Buy ingredients separately at nurseries, mix them by hand, and store the soil for future use. Mix thoroughly, *very* thoroughly, until all ingredients are thoroughly balanced. My recipe for soil mix is equal parts of sand, garden loam, and compost, to which I add a handful each of bone meal and cottonseed meal and a sprinkling of charcoal and perlite.

You can mix soil in a bucket or a bushel. It is quite a job and a messy one, so do it on a porch or outdoors, if possible. If you do not have these areas, buy packaged soil as it comes and just add a little compost, bone meal, and cottonseed meal to each pot.

LIGHT AND AIR

Light is vital to plant growth; without some light no plant (no matter what kind) will grow. Light is necessary for the process of photosynthesis, which transforms elements into plant food. Some crops need more light than others; the small fruits, for example, require very good light to thrive. However, root crops such as radishes and carrots can get along fine with only bright light and no sun, and leafy vegetables such as lettuce and chard will grow in less than bright light. Just how you define light in and around your home is important, so let us describe light levels to help you help your plants.

Only leafy crops will be able to withstand low light levels—places away from windows—and even here there should be enough light, say enough to read by. This light is considered subdued or filtered light. Near windows, that is, on sills or tables below windows, the light level will be quite bright at south and west exposures; this is good bright light where many plants can grow, including fruit trees, which need the most light. Your east and north exposures will give some light but not as bright or as intense as the other exposures. These are the places for carrots and radishes, or some herbs.

If you want very sunny light for your plants, you will have to have them close to the glass, which means window shelves or perhaps a small window greenhouse (there are many available today). In such sunny windows you can grow practically any plant and it will prosper. Forget dark corners or any other shady place; plants simply will not grow. If your place is dark, you must supply artificial light, as explained in Chapter 4.

Light levels at any location vary with the seasons. In summer light

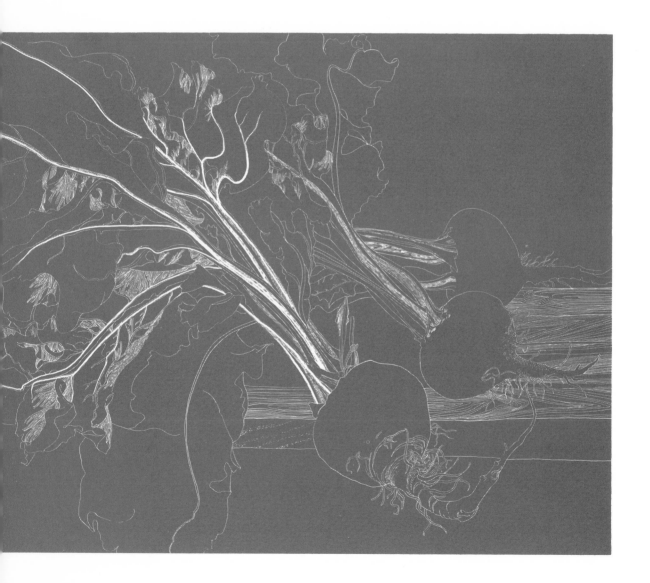

is brighter than in winter, and although you may not be sensitive to these levels, plants are. In winter, when light is at a premium, some artificial light to supplement natural light is a good idea, for example, an incandescent lamp nearby.

Air—a good circulation of air—is necessary for vegetables, herbs, or fruit trees. No plant likes a stuffy, stagnant air situation. Furthermore, a good circulation of air discourages insects from attacking plants. A small electric fan at low speed can do a lot to keep your plants healthy. Place it in the growing area, and on very warm, stagnant, summer days keep it going.

WATERING AND FEEDING

Vegetables, herbs, and fruit trees can take a great deal of water; indeed, they must have thorough watering to really grow. Sparse watering, that is, wetting only part of the soil, will result in pockets of dry soil where roots cannot get water; eventually the plant will die. Always soak plants when watering; every particle of soil should be moist, and excess water should come out the bottom of the container. Water is absolutely necessary to carry food to plants, and without it you will have a sparse harvest. Remember that plants are on a liquid diet and water is their lifeline.

Thorough watering means you will need some facility for catching excess water. Use saucers and bins, or once a week take plants to the sink and soak them to within 1 inch of the pot rim to keep soil really moist. Again, remember that vegetables must grow rapidly without stop to produce a good crop.

Keeping the soil moist is very important, but it is equally important not to drown plants because if you get too much water, there is no oxygen in the soil; oxygen is needed to maintain healthy plant growth. The roots must not drown, so what is needed is an evenly moist soil. This comes only with experience. There are no set rules. You must observe and experiment until you come up with the proper watering schedule.

Plants must have nitrogen, phosphorus, and potassium to grow well. These elements are in soil, but most plants use them up quickly, so they

must be replaced. Replacing them is known as feeding. Feeding is the biggest headache to many people when caring for their plants because there are so many plant foods available that it becomes a problem to figure out which ones to use. There are liquid plant foods, soluble plant foods, plant food granules, plant foods for foliage feeding, and so forth. The soluble plant foods are mixed with water according to directions on the bottle; the granular plant foods are scattered on soil and then water is added; and foliage plant foods are mixed and sprayed on leaves—these you do not need. The liquid form is the best. Plant foods also come in many strengths, some high in nitrogen and low in potassium, or some low in nitrogen and high in phosphorus. The contents of plant foods are on the bottle marked in numbers, for example, 10-10-5. Nitrogen is first, phosphorus second, and potassium third; this order does not vary. But rather than getting mired in numbers, use a 20-20-5 plant food for leafy vegetables; 10-20-10 for crops such as carrots and beets; and for all other plants, including fruit trees and herbs, use the standard all-purpose 10-10-5.

You want your plants to have food, but you do not want them to be overfed because this will kill them just as underfeeding will not help them. For most plants use a weak solution every other watering during the growing season. Start feeding plants a few weeks after the final transplant, and continue on a regular program. Remember that with feeding you must also keep soil evenly moist. Feeding alone will not make plants grow; water, again, is essential.

TENDER LOVING CARE

To me, tender loving care means keeping plants healthy. If you follow only half the suggestions just outlined, the plants will grow. The real test of TLC is to keep plants free from insects and diseases that can quickly mow down a garden. Like people, plants catch things from other plants, and once insects get a foothold they keep moving from one plant to the next.

Insects

The first line of defense is observation. If you see a few aphids or mealybugs, you can eradicate them quickly without much trouble. But once they get a foothold you are in trouble; sprays, chemicals, and all other kinds of insidious means will be necessary to save your plants. Prevention is nine-tenths the battle of keeping plants healthy, so be alert and on guard.

What do you look for? Insects! Most common insect pests are discernible by the human eye; it is just a question of spotting them.

Aphids are tiny, oval, soft-bodied pests; mealybugs are cottony masses hard to miss; scale are hard-shelled insects that attach themselves to plants and somewhat resemble apple seeds. All these insects are easy to see and easy to get rid of if you catch them early. The one insect you will not be able to see that is liable to attack plants is spider mite; you must hope that your plants are not attacked by this culprit. Dry air is a common cause of spider mite, so be forewarned.

In addition to the insects just mentioned, vegetables (depending upon the kind) will attract other unwanted visitors, although they may never appear if you keep a clean house. Chewing insects of various kinds love leafy vegetables, so keep rotenone insecticide on hand. Hookworms and cutworms may appear on tomatoes, but do not panic; hand pick them and destroy them, or use Sevin (only one or two applications are needed). Cucumber beetles are easily discouraged from squash and cucumbers by using a regular rotenone or pyrethrum insecticide. If you are growing beans, be on the alert for bean leaf beetles or Mexican bean beetles.

Squash borers are nefarious critters, and I hate them because I love squash. These insects can wipe out a good crop; if you see them, dust with rotenone, especially in early June to about mid-July. Two serious tomato diseases—verticillium and fusarium—may attack, so have on hand necessary remedies (available in packages at nurseries).

Last, but certainly not least, snails and slugs like vegetables almost as much as people do. Get snail and slug bait; Corys is the best if you can find it, but if not, try Buggeta. Sprinkle pellets on the soil. Use these chemicals and all insecticides with care and only as detailed on the package. It is especially important in any type of vegetable garden to observe caution on labels about discontinuing use a certain length of time before harvest.

Diseases

Diseases rarely attack plants in container growing. However, in the yard some of the common diseases such as blight, bacterial spot, and fusarium wilt may occur. Again, do not panic because there are some excellent preventatives. But like insects that have favorite foods, diseases attack certain crops too. [Many vegetable varieties are not disease-resistant; look for the kinds that are because they are certainly worth the search.]

The following charts will help you to identify insects and the damage they inflict, and diseases and cures. The information is general because the subject of insects is so enormous that space does not permit us to discuss everything. For further information, write for

These tomatoes have been infected with bacterial wilt; a fungicide would have prevented this. (Photo USDA)

USDA Bulletin No. 163, "Minigardens for Vegetables," 15 cents, available from: Superintendent of Documents, Government Printing Office, Washington, D.C. 20250.

INSECT*	DESCRIPTION	VEGETABLE	DAMAGE
Aphids	Soft-bodied sucking insects; green, red, black	All vegetables	Stems and leaves eaten
Bean leaf beetles	Reddish beetles with black spots	Beans	Circular holes
Cabbage worms	Green larvae	Cabbage	Holes in leaves
Cabbage maggots	Small, legless, white maggots near soil	Broccoli, turnips	Plants stunted
Corn borers	Small, pale-colored larvae	Corn	Stalks and ears tunneled
Corn earworms	Green or brown larvae	Corn	Kernels destroyed, silk cut
Cucumber beetles, Diabrotica	Spotted or striped beetles	Cucumber, squash	Leaves eaten
Mexican bean beetles	Copper-colored beetles with many spots	Beans	Eaten leaves, almost skeletonized
Rust flys	White maggots at root	Carrots	Crown and roots eaten
Slugs and snails	Easily recognizable	All vegetables	Eaten leaves and fruit
Squash bugs	Brownish flat bugs	Squash	Plants wilt, yellow
Squash vine borers	Cannot be seen	Squash	Sudden wilting
Striped or spotted cucumber beetles	Brown beetles	Cucumbers, summer squash	Plants eaten
Tomato hookworms	Green worms	Tomatoes	Leaves eaten
Tomato cutworms	Dark-colored cutworms	Tomatoes	Fruit eaten

Most of these insects can be controlled with Sevin or pyrethrum.

VEGETABLE	DISEASE	SYMPTOMS
Beans	Bacterial blight	Water-soaked spots on leaves
Beans	Anthracnose	Dark reddish areas on leaves
Cabbage Cauliflower Broccoli	Fusarium yellow	Leaves turn yellow, then curl
Carrot, Parsnip	Leaf blight	Leaves turn yellow, then brown
Corn	Blight	Streaks, spots
Cucumbers Squash	Anthracnose	Round reddish brown or black spots on leaves
Peas	Bacterial wilt Fusarium wilt Blight	Vines rapidly wither Plants stunted, yellow Colored dark streaks on stems, round dark spots on leaves
Tomato	Powdery mildew	Grayish powdery coating
Pepper	Blight (early, late)	Brown to black spots on leaves, water-soaked areas
Eggplant	Wilt Bacterial spot	Plants stunted Greasy spots, yellow margins on leaves

Fungicide preventatives are at local nurseries. Once you have diagnosed the disease from this chart get the appropriate remedy.

Note: When using any insecticide or fungicide check label to determine when to stop spraying before harvest (generally it is two to three weeks).

GETTING VEGETABLES STARTED

There are two ways to start your vegetables: Buy seed in packages at local nurseries and supermarkets, then sow seed (not as difficult as you think). Or buy seedlings, (pre-started plants) at nurseries at appropriate times. The first method is less expensive, yields more, and has an advantage in that you can have any kind of vegetable variety you want rather than what is for sale. The latter way is for people who want fresh vegetables (a few) but do not have time to start them themselves. Either way, you will be far better off than buying produce from markets. Many vegetables, for example, tomatoes and cucumbers, are available as pre-planted plants at nurseries at appropriate times to the locale. The advantage here is that the plants have gone through the crucial germination time and are already growing, so it is merely a matter of removing the seedlings with as much of the root ball intact as possible and putting them in fresh soil in new containers. Beets and carrots are not generally available pre-started because they are so easily grown from seed, even by the novice.

Herbs deserve special consideration because now there are many prepackaged kits; all you do is lift the plastic wrapper, add water, and put plants in suitable light. This method seems good, but it is expensive, and you have to be a pretty good gardener to nurture the little seeds into plants. Variety is limited too. So start your own from seed for the best results (see Chapter 9).

Dwarf fruit trees are sold at nurseries in cans. It is a better idea to buy the started plant rather than nurturing an orange tree to maturity, which takes some years. Starting fruit trees from seed is for professionals, so buy your dwarf peaches and citrus from local suppliers (see Chapter 8).

STARTING FROM SEED

Sowing

Starting your own plants from seed really frightens people, but I do not know why. It is an easy method, with all the odds in your favor. Each seed packet contains many seeds, and some are bound to sprout even if ignored. Vegetable seed packets are sold at garden shops and nurseries and even at hardware and variety stores. The selection is limited, but if you want only a few radishes or lettuce, this is an acceptable way to start. If you want your own chosen varieties, order from the many seed suppliers throughout the country. Catalogs are sent in winter, so you will have plenty of time to pick and choose for early spring planting. And when you order from mail suppliers you have the advantage of getting the many new varieties, such as midget varieties, *especially developed for container gardening.*

Some seed can be sown directly into the container in which they will mature; other seed is best started in containers or flats, to be transplanted later. The instructions on the packet give this information. Just what you put your seeds in depends upon what is available. Do not go and buy special containers; even the standard clay pot you have around the house will accommodate many seeds. Or use household items as previously mentioned such as the aluminum trays frozen rolls come in or milk cartons cut lengthwise. The important thing is

Left: *Starting vegetables from seed can be done in a vermiculite and soil mix in a shallow container; here a wooden box is used.* (Photo by author)

Right: *Pre-started plants (from nurseries) can be transplanted into large tubs to grow on for harvest.* (Photo by author)

that the container has drainage holes so excess water can escape. Put a small layer of pea gravel on the bottom of the container to facilitate good drainage. Sow the seed on standard seed-sowing mediums—soil, vermiculite, perlite; these come packaged at nurseries. The main thing is to use a sterile medium. Some seed can be merely placed on the soil and then covered with a thin coating of soil, but larger seeds have to be buried into the soil to the depth of the seed (see chart at end of chapter). The directions on the packet will tell you spacing, but it is best to use *more* seeds than advised because generally these directions are for outdoor sowing rather than indoor gardening.

Once the seeds are in place and watered, put four sticks, one at each end of the container, about 4 inches high, to hold the plastic tent (a Baggie) that should now be put on top of the container to ensure good humidity for seed germination. Place the seed container in a warm (check seed packets for germination temperatures), bright place but with no direct sun. Do not water the seeds again until they sprout. Indeed, check daily to see if the growing medium is too moist; too much moisture causes mildew, the bane of all gardeners. If the soil is too wet, remove the plastic and let the seeds dry out in a bright, sunny place for a few hours.

Water the transplanted seedlings thoroughly with a fine mist. Do it two or three times until all soil settles and is thoroughly moist so the tiny plant roots have an ample supply of the moisture that is essential

for growth. Move the new plants to a bright window in warmth, or put them under artificial light.

There are now many ways to start seeds. For example, you can use peat pots or peat cubes; add the seed and start as directed above. The advantage is that you do not have to repot and uproot the plant at transplanting time; you simply pot peat pot and all. You can also use compressed peat-started disks. You put the seed into the disk and water it; the disk swells up. Some disks already contain seeds. Also available are seed tapes for outdoor gardens. Just plant the tape, which already holds the seed.

No matter which method you use, the main objective is to see that the plant gets good humidity, air, light, and water so it can grow

Vegetables Under Lights

uninterrupted. If you allow the small seedlings to become bone dry for even a day, that is the end of your garden.

When the seedlings are up (in their permanent pots), you can move them outdoors to grow on a porch or balcony, or put them at the window. In either case, do not just set them into intense sun; allow them to get used to it by putting them in bright light for a few hours each day for several days before they are in their permanent places. Fertilize vegetables to keep them growing well. Use plant foods (as described in chapter 3) every other watering for best results.

Seeds Under Artificial Light

If natural light is limited at home, do not give up the idea of having a few vegetables. Use artificial light. Seeds germinate beautifully under fluorescent light, and they prosper in such situations because you are working with controlled light. (Recent reports in many periodicals indicate that plants started under lights are often superior to those grown in greenhouses.) Sturdy seedlings are produced when the amount of red exceeds the far-red light. With higher levels of red the seedlings tend to grow greener and shorter, with well-developed leaves and stems. Fluorescent lamps should be used for early seedlings because incandescent lamps have a high level of far-red radiation that opposes the effect of red light and is thus not desirable for seedlings.

Artificial-light gardening takes little space; you can do it in the basement or even in a pantry or closet if you like. You can make your own wooden tray or bin units and add commercial artificial-light fixtures, or buy commercial ready-made table models or carts. Although there are dozens of new kinds of fluorescent lights made especially for plant growing, the standard warm-white daylight fluorescent tubes sold at most hardware stores will work fine and are cheaper. So do not be too concerned about fancy apparatus or equipment.

For germinating seeds under artificial light, use 10 lamp watts per square foot of growing area. For example, four 40-watt, 48-inch fluorescent lamps will work fine. Cover the seeds *very* lightly with the propagating mix. Then comb or scrape the surface somewhat after soaking the medium to allow better penetration of light and to permit oxygen to enter the seeds. For good seed germination, generally keep the temperature at about 78°F. (Some seeds require lower temperatures, some higher, but 78°F. is the optimum for most seeds.) If possible, use a heating cable (at suppliers) in the bottom of the container to keep temperature constant and warm.

Keep seeds about 4 to 6 inches from light source, with light on from 14 to 16 hours a day. When germination starts, move the seedlings closer to the lamps, say, 4 inches. Light duration can remain the same.

Artificial light units, shown here in a commercial display, provide an excellent way to start vegetable seed at home. When plants are large enough they are transplanted to garden or pot. (Photo courtesy GTE Sylvania)

Here is the proper size and stage of growth of a tomato plant for planting. (Photo USDA)

When putting plants in the ground try to include as much of the root ball as possible; this eliminates disturbing the roots and plants grow better. (Photo USDA)

When seedlings are large enough to handle, they can be transferred to individual pots or set in the yard. Remember, however, to keep thinning before this step.

Thinning and Transplanting

The time needed for plants to sprout varies with each plant; some come up in a week, and others may take a month. When seedlings are

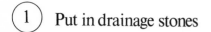

② Add potting soil

③ Carefully plant young sprout in soil

④ When plant matures tie stake to stalk for added support

Starting Vegetables

up and you can see green growth, remove the plastic tent and move the container to a bright location. Mist the soil with water if it needs it. As the seedlings unfold leaves you will see them crowding each other; now is the time to thin out the batch. Remove some of the weaker leaves so stronger ones have space to grow. Thin the crop with a tiny scissors, a pencil, or any blunt-edged instrument; never just rip the seedlings out because this will disturb the root system of the other plants. When these seedlings show four to six true leaves, move them to larger quarters. The larger containers can be clay pots, wooden flats, and so on. Remove the seedlings carefully, trying to get as much of the root ball intact with soil as possible to minimize the shock of transplanting. The new container for your young plants should be clean and have drainage shards (pieces of pots) at the bottom. It should also contain a good rich potting soil, one that has plenty of nutrients, so plants can grow readily. Packaged soils are available, or you might want to mix your own, as described in the previous chapter.

TIME GUIDE FOR VEGETABLE GROWING

VEGETABLE	CONTAINER SIZE (INCHES)	BUY PLANT (BP) OR SEED DEPTH (INCHES)	WS*	CS†	SIZE MATURE (INCHES)	DAYS FROM SEED TO HARVEST
Beans (bush)	8–10	1	X		24	50–55
Beets	10–12	1–2		X	12	50–60
Carrots	10–12	½		X	12	70–75
Corn, sweet	Planter beds	½	X		24–36	75–90
Cucumber	10–12	1	X		24–36	50
Eggplant	12–14	BP	X		21–36	50–55
Endive	h.p.‡	¼		X	2–4	95
Escarole	h.p.	¼		X	2–4	85
Lettuce	h.p.	½		X	10	20–40
Peas	Planter beds	1		X	24–30	65–75
Pepper	10–12	BP	X		12–24	115
Radish	6–8	½		X	6–8	20–30
Spinach	8–10	½–1		X	2–4	50–60
Squash	16–20	1	X		24–36	60–65
Swiss Chard	10–20	1		X	12	75
Tomato	8–10	BP	X		24–36	100–120

*WS = warm-season vegetable.
†CS = cool-season vegetable.
‡h.p. = hanging planter.

VEGETABLES IN THE SKY

Because of today's overcrowded city conditions, rooftop gardening is enjoying a renaissance. This is a unique and pleasant way for many people who otherwise could not enjoy the soil to have small gardens. Even an apartment dweller can, with some neighbors, use the rooftop (after getting permission from the landlord) to grow vegetables or fruit trees. Practically any roof can be used, but some knowledge of rooftop gardening is necessary if you want to be successful, for in the air plants are subject to intense heat and sun, wind and pollution, and these conditions must be overcome.

STARTING THE ROOFTOP GARDEN

Before you start your rooftop farm, be sure the roof can support the weight of soil and plants and there are ample drainage facilities for water to escape easily. Generally most roofs can take the weight and the excess water, but it is always prudent to be sure. Check to see that there are no leaks or cracks; if so, some asphalt repair may be

On roof garden and terraces there is plenty of sun to grow many kinds of crops. Container gardening is a popular and easy way to have plants in crowded cities. (Photo by Barr)

necessary before you start. Be sure there are drain tiles connected to outlets so water escapes and does not accumulate on the roof and cause damage to the structure. Check that railings are in place; peoples' safety must be considered.

Most roof gardens have blustery winds that can dry plants quickly or blow them to pieces, so try to incorporate some type of fencing or barrier against prevailing winds. Erect simple but secure board fences, and if necessary, use some slatted canopies to break the intense noon sun so plants do not burn.

You can certainly dump soil on a roof and start gardening, but it is much more intelligent to have soil in contained planter beds (for vegetables) or in large pots (for fruit trees). Even if you are not handy, you can nail together a bed of rough redwood boards. Make

Planter boxes such as these can accommodate vegetables nicely on rooftops where growing conditions are ideal for sun-loving crops. (Photo by Barr)

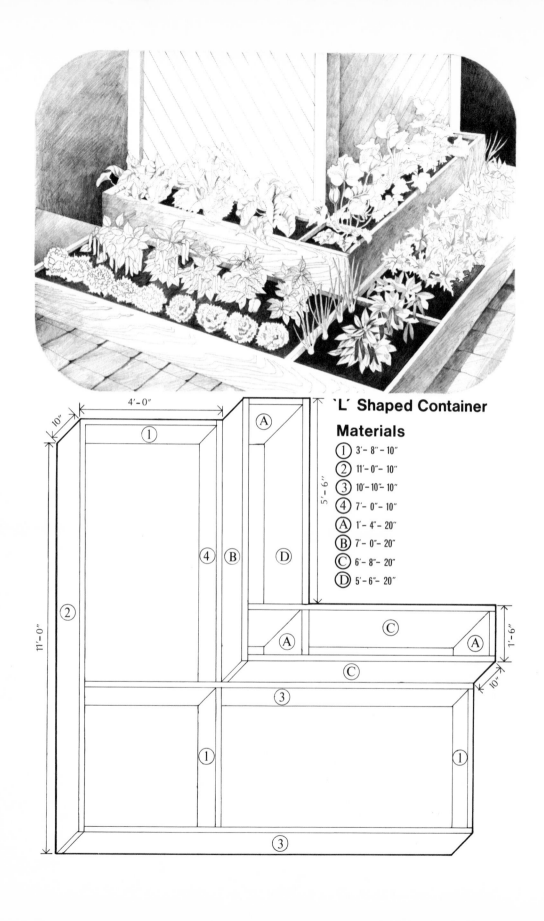

'L' Shaped Container

Materials

①	3′– 8″– 10″
②	11′– 0″– 10″
③	10′– 10″– 10″
④	7′– 0″– 10″
Ⓐ	1′– 4″– 20″
Ⓑ	7′– 0″– 20″
Ⓒ	6′– 8″– 20″
Ⓓ	5′– 6″– 20″

the bed about 5 x 10 feet; this should furnish enough produce for several people. Also, use trellises or unique fence designs to create beauty and a place for vining vegetables like squash and cucumbers. Plant vegetables to the same depths as those discussed in the next chapter (Backyard Gardening).

As mentioned, use large ornamental pots for fruit trees, and place trees in sun with some protection from wind. Wind increases evaporation in plants, which causes rapid desiccation and injury to soft young leaves. Do not enclose all sides; determine the windiest areas and use buffers there.

WHAT YOU CAN GROW

Although you can grow many kinds of vegetables, do not be a dreamer and think you can have corn or asparagus from your city farm. Generally you cannot because they take too much work, as do broccoli and cauliflower. And if you work every day, there simply will not be time. Weekend gardening is not for vegetables; they need a good deal of attention on rooftops. So select the easy ones like tomatoes and lettuce, squash and eggplant, beets and such that will give you a profusion of harvest.

You can start your vegetables inside to get a head start on spring, or start planting in mid-March, April, or May, depending upon your locale (when killing frosts are over), directly into the soil. Try to stay with the miniature varieties described in this book because they yield as much as their larger cousins and do not take up much space. If you are starting vegetables inside, at transplanting time slowly acclimatize them to the outdoors. Take them outside for a couple of hours the first day, longer the second day, and finally leave them out overnight so they gradually become used to outdoor conditions.

Four or five tubs of the many dwarf fruit trees available—oranges, peaches—will give you fresh luscious fruit. Herbs too can be grown on the rooftop in the smallest of space, and once established they will fend for themselves. Select the herbs you like, whatever they may be; plant them directly in the soil to have fresh, wonderful seasoning.

CARE OF THE ROOFTOP LARDER

With outdoor conditions your plants will need copious watering and the best potting soil you can get. Use a very rich friable potting soil that is porous and has all necessary nutrients. In the city, getting soil is a chore, and using small packs (called hobby packs) will make you broke. Instead, try to talk your nursery or florist into letting you buy soil by the bushel from his stock. Many florists have bulk soil. If you cannot find this kind of soil, consider buying it by mail. It sounds

expensive, but it is not half as expensive as hobby sacks; a 60-pound bale of soil runs about ten dollars, shipping included.

Vegetables are heavy feeders, so be sure you have plenty of fertilizer on hand and feed plants every other watering. Use a mild fertilizer such as 10-10-5 for good results. Also, mix some compost (now available in tidy sacks) into the soil. (Making your own compost is not for city dwellers; it takes too much time and trouble.) Include some packaged manure in the soil because many vegetables—cucumbers and squash, for example—need it to prosper. You do not have to follow livestock

around the city; simply buy packaged manure, or buy by mail order if you cannot find it anywhere nearby.

For the umpteenth time, remember that vegetables (and fruit trees and herbs) need water, water, water. This does not mean a light sprinkling every day, but rather a thorough soaking at least twice a week, more often if you have time. Keep weeds down or they will sop the nutrients plants need from soil. Hand weed (good exercise) or use mulches (stone, firbark) between vegetables. Above all, do not use any lethal weed killer! You can also use black plastic between vegetables to keep weeds out. Weight down plastic with pebbles. This works fine for me. And be sure to be alert to insect attacks. Yes, insects do live in the city, and you will have your share of borers and cutworms. However, insects need not upset you or the vegetables. Pyrethrum and rotenone, two natural insecticides, are available in packages; used on a regular schedule according to package directions, they should keep your salad greens free of insects. Multipurpose vegetable insecticides are also available, and some have a fungicide as well mixed in to combat fungus disease. Sevin is used frequently; again, follow packaged directions carefully and to the letter. (See charts in Chapter 3.)

Any of the vegetables, fruit trees, and herbs discussed in this book are fine for the rooftop garden. My favorites include beets, carrots, lettuce, squash, tomatoes, eggplant, and peppers, along with Bonanza Peach and an assortment of seasoning herbs.

VEGETABLES IN THE BACKYARD GARDEN

The person with even a small backyard, or someone else's backyard he has to share, can have a productive vegetable garden that will not only save money but will also offer a chance to grow and have some of the more unusual gourmet vegetables. There are several new ways to approach the vegetable garden, so forget about all old advice. You will generally be growing in a limited area, perhaps 10 x 20 feet (and that is room enough). Or you might want to try vertical farming if you really lack space (and this method is a space saver). Peas, cucumbers, pole beans, and tomatoes can all be grown on vertical trellises in very confined space. You can also go ahead and be adventurous and use beets, spinach, or cabbage as border edging for flower beds. There is a whole new world of vegetable gardening out there once you get started.

HOW TO APPROACH IT

First, do not try to grow everything and anything; be selective and choose easy vegetables that will give you a high yield without too much work. This means lettuce, spinach, beets, and carrots. Forget about vegetables like squash, which run rampant and must be picked almost every day once they are mature. Brussels sprouts and cabbage take a good deal of work and space too, so keep to the midget varieties or those kinds of vegetables that are easy to work with.

A 10 x 20-foot garden plot will give you enough vegetables for a family of six (with some to spare) for the entire summer. Again, as with all vegetable gardening, the idea is to get the cool-season vege-

This lovely backyard garden provides plenty of space for vegetables for the whole family. Included are beans, lettuce, and eggplant. (Photo by J. Wilson)

tables started at the right time and the warm growers in after frosts. (See chart at end of Chapter 4.)

As mentioned in Chapter 4, some vegetables can be sown directly into the ground (this information is marked on back of packets); other vegetables must be started indoors first or in cold frames outdoors and then transplanted later.

To get your mini-garden going, start improving the soil. This does not mean killing yourself hauling in tons of soil and compost; it merely means an afternoon of spading and digging to make sure the soil is porous. Vegetables will not grow in claylike or sandy soils. In claylike soil, water cannot get to vegetables, and in a sandy soil water leaches away so fast it is of no use to the plants. So add some organic matter (compost if you have it) to the soil, or buy it or manure and add about

Many different kinds of vegetables are grown in this backyard. Plants in various stages of growth are shown. (Photo USDA)

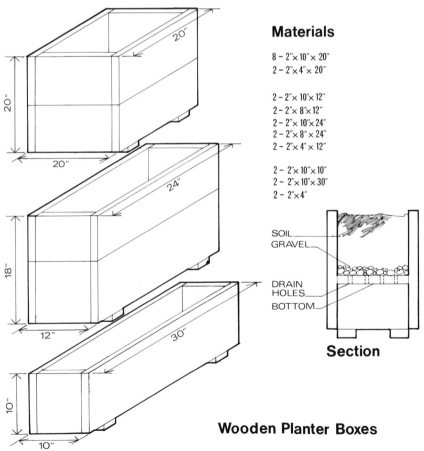

Materials

8 – 2"× 10"× 20"
2 – 2"× 4"× 20"

2 – 2"× 10"× 12"
2 – 2"× 8"× 12"
2 – 2"× 10"× 24"
2 – 2"× 8"× 24"
2 – 2"× 4"× 12"

2 – 2"× 10"× 10"
2 – 2"× 10"× 30"
2 – 2"× 4"

SOIL
GRAVEL

DRAIN
HOLES
BOTTOM

Section

Wooden Planter Boxes

a 2-inch layer. Also spread a 10-10-5 plant food into the soil and rake it into the top few inches of soil. Now rake again.

For cool-weather vegetables, get seeds in the ground; plant them about three times the depth of the diameter of the seed. Plant small seeds like carrots shallow, large seeds like peas deeper. To keep a straight furrow, use a taut string strung across the garden on a wooden stake. Drop seed in place along the row, and tamp soil in place. When all early crops are in the ground, mist soil until it is evenly damp.

Remember that cool-weather crops like cabbages and onions, carrots and beets can be planted as soon as ground is workable. Plant tomatoes, peppers, and beans only after the danger of frost is over. To transplant seedlings or pre-started vegetables, dig a hole with a trowel for each plant and then insert the plant and firm the soil around the collar.

Beets, radishes, carrots, and lettuce need to be thinned when they are about 3 inches high to allow more growing space. Cut thinnings; do not pull them out. Beans and peas need no thinning; squash and cucumbers need some but never drastic thinning until they are 6 inches tall.

GROWING VEGETABLES

Water and sun are the secrets of good vegetable growing; plants need buckets of water and at least 4 to 5 hours of daily sun. When you water, soak plants, do not just sprinkle them, and if possible, water in the morning so plants are dry before nightfall to avoid fungus diseases. Adequate watering improves the resistance of the plants and helps prevent drought-related problems such as tomato blight.

Feed plants every other watering. If insects or diseases attack your vegetables, do not panic. Use the same preventatives as described in Chapter 3, remembering to persevere and use them frequently and exactly according to directions on the package. If you prefer organic gardening, import ladybugs (they are available by mail) and release them in the garden. Or use old-fashioned remedies like hand-picking bugs, or a mixture of laundry soap and water followed by a thorough rinsing, to eliminate pests. Remember that for vegetables to be fresh and tasty they must be grown quickly and without stopping, which means plenty of water and moderate feedings to get rapid growth. Be sure weeds (mentioned in Chapter 5) do not sap strength from soil that your vegetables need. Hand pick weeds or use mulches between plants to keep weeds down.

Some Hints

Plant fast-growing vegetables like lettuce between slow growers like cabbage. Use succession planting, that is, cool-weather crops like

The beauty of escarole both for viewing and for eating is evident in this closeup photo. (Photo by J. Wilson)

peas followed by warm-weather beans, to get the most out of the land. Be sure to keep space between vegetables free of weeds. Hand pick weeds when you see them, not days later. Try to plant as closely as possible.

Here are some specific hints on vegetables to get your bounty going:

BEETS: Grow beets quickly, and pick them when they are young. Give them buckets of water when they are showing good growth. Try Detroit Dark Red for a resistant variety.

CABBAGE: This is a tough crop and takes space. It is also subject to chewing insects, so be prepared. Hand pick any worms. Use rotenone when necessary. Harvest when heads are solid.

CARROTS: These are slow to germinate, so do not panic if you do not see green for a while. Once carrots start, thin them or the crop will be sparse.

LETTUCE: If you want good lettuce yield, cool weather is the secret. Keep picking lettuce to get more.

PEAS: Start only in cool weather. Use peas fast; pick them as soon as pods are firm.

PEPPERS: Frost quickly kills peppers, so be forewarned; be sure weather is stable before you put plants out. You can harvest peppers at any size.

RADISHES: These are the easiest vegetables to grow; they do not need any special care.

Here, lettuce is ready for plucking; in the backyard it is one step to the kitchen and a crisp salad. (Photo by J. Wilson)

SPINACH: You can start spinach in early spring or in late fall. Keep picking spinach; never let plants go to seed.

SQUASH: If you want squash, use the bush type; the others take too much space. Pick squash when young and tender. Borers may attack squash, so be on the alert and dust plants with rotenone in June and July.

TOMATOES: Stake tomatoes: Tie the plants to wooden stakes with soft string. Remove suckers that develop in axils of main leaf stalks. If tomato hornworm attacks, use the chemical Sevin. Pick tomatoes as soon as they are red; green picked tomatoes ripened indoors will not have good flavor.

A BUSHEL
OF VEGETABLES

Large plots of land are not necessary for your vegetable garden. As mentioned in Chapter 1, you can have fresh produce and an adequate supply in bushel baskets, wooden planters, and so on. And, with just five or six containers you can grow an ample supply of vegetables for your family. Beans and beets, carrots and lettuce are well within the scope of even the smallest apartment dweller. Tomatoes are a favorite of many people, and fresh lettuce is always welcomed at home. What follows are some of the easier vegetables to grow in and around the house. I have mentioned some named varieties because they perform well in almost any situation, but this is not a complete list because every year new plants suitable to container growing and for the person with limited space are developed. In any case, always try to select disease-resistant varieties if they are available.

BEANS

Bush beans and wax beans are a nutritional food, and new varieties are available for the apartment dweller to grow. These mature in 60 days. The container should be at least 28 inches long, 8 inches wide, and about 8 inches deep. This size will fit a windowsill or can be accommodated on a balcony or patio. The dwarf varieties tend to be hardier and more robust than other beans. The plants require good warmth and lots of water and fertilizer, especially when they begin to form pods. Use a 10-10-5 fertilizer and grow about six plants—that is all you will need. You can repeat sowing for continuous crops. Pick the beans while they are young, and before the seeds begins to swell the pods, to ensure good flavor and encourage productivity. Good varieties include

Burpee Golden Beet

Blue Lake Bush Bean
Bush Romano Bean
Henderson Bush
Honey Gold Wax Bean
Sprite Bush Bean
Tenderpod

Pole snap beans can also be grown on trellises or fences where space is limited. They produce over a long period and require the same care as Bush Beans. Try

Kentucky Wonder
Romano

BEETS

Beets are full of good nutrition and can be used for salads or as a cooked vegetable. The tops too can be eaten lightly boiled and salted. All in all, beets make a fabulous home crop. The seeds can be planted directly in large containers of soil. When they are about 2 inches high, thin them so the plants are about 1 inch apart. When they reach 8 or 9 inches, thin them again by removing every other plant, leaving 3-inch spaces between plants. Harvest beets early; if left too long they become pithy and lose flavor. Small beets have excellent taste.

Beets like a cool temperature and do not want excessive heat, so put them in a shady, somewhat cool place, perhaps a doorway or porch. If plants heave out of the soil in the pot, merely add some fresh soil. Keep plants evenly moist; like most vegetables, beets like plenty of water. Many varieties are available, including

Ruby Queen
Detroit Dark Red
Burpees Golden Beet

CABBAGE, CAULIFLOWER, BROCCOLI

These vegetables require a lot of space, and although you can grow one cabbage plant, say, to a 12-inch tub, it really is not worth it. Even the small backyard or rooftop is generally not large enough to really

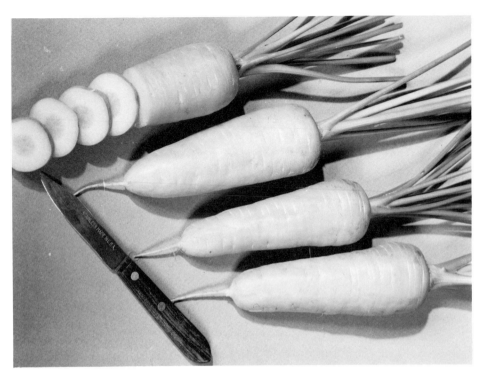

Goldinhart Carrot

accommodate these crops. Furthermore, cauliflower, broccoli, and cabbage are too demanding and take a lot of care and time. They are inevitably attacked by insects, which is more trouble to the average gardener, who is not around all week. For these reasons I suggest buying these vegetables at your supermarket. No, the taste will not be as good as home-grown kinds, but you cannot have everything!

CARROTS

If carrots taste tasteless to you, no wonder. Those you buy at the market are weeks old, and there is an incredible difference in home-grown types. Especially to my liking are the fine baby carrots (not available in markets) because they are very sweet and tender. Carrots need a very friable, open soil to prosper. Rapid growth is necessary, so frequent feeding and ample water is a prime consideration. The longer it takes to mature the more pithy the carrot will be, which is hardly desirable. Because carrots now come in many lengths, from 3 to 15 inches, be sure to use the proper container to accommodate the plants.

Sow carrot seed in spring or fall, and do not fret if it takes a while; many varieties do not germinate for 3 or 4 weeks. More important than with any other vegetable, carrots need good humidity to germinate, so use the plastic tent method described in Chapter 4. Plant two rows of carrots, and thin them when they are about 2 inches tall. Thin the plants again in about a month. Most varieties require about 70 days to become mature. You can resow after harvesting if you want more carrots. Try the following varieties

Tiny Sweet
Short N' Sweet
Nantes
Baby Finger Nantes

CORN

Corn seems to be everyone's favorite, and there is little argument that fresh corn in taste far exceeds corn bought at the market. The first rule for good sweet corn, or any corn for that matter, is never plant in one row. Corn is wind-pollinated, so it must be planted in three or four rows. For our use the variety called Golden Midget can be grown in large planters planted in blocks of three or four. Sow seed directly in soil, and when they are up thin them so they are about 3 inches apart. If you are planting outdoors plant seed 2 inches deep in rows about 30 inches apart; later thin to 10 to 14 inches apart. There are early, mid-season, and late varieties of corn, so do successive plantings if you want corn from summer into fall.

Watering and good hot weather (although some varieties that require less heat are now available) are what do the job. Some gardeners remove suckers, but others do not. I am one of the latter and have found little difference. Remember not to overcrowd corn, and do thin it out or you will have little, if any, crop.

Corn borers and corn earworms are the nemesis of corn. You will have to start dusting crops with Sevin when they are up about 18 inches. The Golden Midget variety matures in only 60 days from seed. Other varieties vary from 65 to 90 days, and because there are so many varieties of corn, no specific suggestions are given here. Choose what does best in your locale by asking your nurseryman.

CUCUMBERS

When I first saw cucumbers in a container on a windowsill of a friend's house, I inspected them carefully to determine what kind of house plant they were. The thought of growing cucumbers indoors was quite new to me. I was amazed and am still rather amused to see tiny delicious cucumbers on plants grown on the patio. The plants are extremely

Meridian Cucumber

robust, grow quickly, and produce a good harvest. You can sow the seed (buy midget varieties) directly into soil in a large 12-inch container. Insert trellises or stakes so the plants can climb. Train the vine so the center becomes bushy and the lateral stems develop sideways.

Give plants plenty of water, and be sure to add some manure to the potting soil. Keep plants in a bright place, but direct sun is not necessary. Cucumbers start bearing in about 40 to 70 days and can be picked at any stage. The young ones will be tiny but ideal for sweet pickles; larger ones, if you let them mature, are fine for salads. Try these varieties

Challenger Hybrid
China Hybrid
Mincu
Triumph F. Hybrid

EGGPLANT

A warm-weather crop, eggplant does best at about 80°F. during the day and 68°F. at night. Start seeds in April or May, depending upon your location, and use peat pots to avoid shock of transplanting, or better yet, buy pre-started plants because eggplant seed is difficult to germinate and needs constant heat (80 to 85°F.). Use somewhat large containers when ready for transplanting, and be ready for a surprise: The plant has beautiful lush leaves. Eggplant needs a long warm growing season, so put them outside when weather is uniformly warm, keeping them well watered and in a bright place.

Plants can be easily trained to a stake or trellis and will grow about 3 or 4 feet, depending upon the variety. Remove some blossoms as they appear so eggplant does not set too many fruits. Pinch back terminal stem growth to keep the plant bushy. Eggplant should bear in about 75 to 90 days; harvest immediately, even when the fruits are half size. If picked too late, the fruit will have a bitter taste. Good eggplant varieties include

Black Magic
Golden Yellow
Morden Midget

ENDIVE AND ESCAROLE

These greens are flavorful, distinctive-tasting vegetables that can be used with lettuce or eaten by themselves as a salad. Like lettuce they are incredibly easy to grow, and two or three plants will furnish ample greens for the family. You can pick leaves as you do with lettuce, or harvest the entire plant when it is mature. Plants need buckets of water and a bright but not sunny spot. Thin them back once or twice to give ample growing space for other seedlings; within 40 to 50 days you should have a good crop of endive or escarole. Use a 10-10-5 fertilizer. Two good varieties are

Full Heart Batavian Escarole
Green Curled Endive

LETTUCE

What is a salad without lettuce? Not much, yet growing your own lettuce is so simple. The loose-head types (leafy ones) are excellent for growing in containers and are ready for plucking within 50 days. Sow the seed where it is to mature, and protect plants against heat. Give them light, but sun is not necessary to ensure the crop. Use about six or eight plants to a container, and resow after harvesting each plant to have a constant succession of good greens. Use a 10-10-5 fertilizer, and give lettuce quantities of water once it is growing. Although maturity time is 50 days, in about a month you can be eating the "thinnings," which are excellent: When lettuce is mature, harvest the outer leaves with a few inner ones at each cutting. Wash and eat; you will be amazed at the flavor.

In addition to being an easy crop to grow, lettuce also makes a very good pot plant. The green leaves are pretty and can be used as a centerpiece in its pot if you want to look and eat at the same time. Here are some good varieties of lettuce

Bibb Lettuce
Buttercrunch
Oak Leaf
Salad Bowl
Tom Thumb Bibb

ONIONS AND CHIVES

Most people are not inclined to grow onions because they are not a popular cooked vegetable dish nor are they overabundantly used in salads. But the home grower is missing a bet if he does not grow scallions (those sweet-tasting green onions), with so many uses, or chives, for seasoning various dishes. These are very easy plants to tend and well worth their space.

You can buy sets or plants of scallions; just set them 1 inch apart in a 10-inch pot. Plants will be ready for eating in about 3 weeks; harvest every other one, giving the others room to grow. Plenty of water and good sun will bring onions into perfection.

Chives hardly need any instruction because they grow so easily and are often seen in little pots at many supermarkets. They are the most agreeable of plants and need only even moisture and good light to keep producing. Simply snip tops of chives to garnish soups, for zesty salads, and for seasoning gravies.

There are really no superior varieties; all seem good, so pick from your mail-order catalog or what is available at stores in your locale.

PEAS

Peas like cool temperatures and are a fairly easy crop to grow, so give them a try. You can get low growing varieties that do not need staking, or trellis types. A fine one is Mighty Midget, which takes little space and matures in 60 days. Little Marvel, a vine type, is also excellent, maturing in about the same time. Sow seed in pots or tubs, about fifteen peas per square foot, and cover with 1 to 2 inches of soil. Germinated peas need plenty of water; later they do not need as much, but still the soil must be moist.

Too hot temperatures will produce all vines, no pods. Watch out for aphids, which cause stunted curly leaves; and pick pods regularly, or pods will become hard.

PEPPERS

Seeds of peppers are difficult to germinate because they require high heat, so buy pre-started plants. These are attractive plants, with dark

Green Pepper

green foliage, and can be easily grown in containers. Peppers, whether the long slender hot peppers or the succulent sweet bell ones, need a warm growing period of about 4 months, with night temperatures never below 65°F. Planting can be started in April or May (depending upon your region).

Some good luck and weather is necessary with peppers because too high temperatures or severe winds will cause blossoms to drop and in very low temperatures plants do not set fruit. Cut off peppers with a knife, leaving a piece of 5 inches; this seems to protect the plant. All red peppers are green until they get ripe, so do not let this confuse you.

Peppers make attractive and bushy 2- to 3-feet-tall plants that are fine decoration for patio, terrace, or porch. Harvest your peppers about

8 to 9 weeks after the first transplanting. Frequent harvesting will encourage production through the summer. Three good varieties are
Italina Sweet
Burgess Michigan Wonder
Canape

RADISHES

Radishes are for the rank beginner because no matter how you grow them they are invariably successful. They grow fast and bear abundantly, two prime requisites for the anxious city gardener. Radishes do not have to be transplanted, and they can be sown in the same container they are to grow in. Even if you are all brown thumbs, you should have a crop within a month.

As a rule radishes do not like hot weather, so it is good to get them going early in spring. If you water plants thoroughly, and I mean water them, the radishes will be crisp and tender. Fertilize the plants when first young leaves appear. How do you tell when radishes are ready? Pick one (you will have some to spare); they should be crisp and succulent, never pithy.

Cherry Belle Radish

Above: *Summer Crookneck Squash* Below: *Zucchini Squash*

The leaves of radishes are rather decorative, so they do add a note of green. You can replace harvested ones with new seed to have a succession of radishes. Named varieties are

Champion Radish
Cherry Belle Radish
Icicle

SPINACH

Spinach does best in cool temperatures; in hot weather it rarely succeeds, although the variety Winter Bloomsdale takes heat better than most spinach types. Not as easy to grow as most vegetables, spinach flowers quickly, which stops production of foliage and thus makes it a failure—this is a day-length problem. Although spinach succeeds in moderate sun, it still needs plenty of water. Most varieties mature in about 40 to 50 days, making spinach a temptation to grow because it is nice to reap a harvest in only 6 or 7 weeks. If you decide to try spinach, look for blight-resistant varieties. Sow seed in tubs or boxes, using two or three seeds per inch of space, and cover with ½ inch of soil. Thin to 3 inches apart when plants start their growth. Excellent varieties are

America
Winter Bloomsdale

SQUASH

Squash produce quite a bumper crop of bushy, compact, and handsome plants. You will end up with too many because squash outgrow their eating time in a few days. Try to pick your squash when they are still small and have the most flavor; left to grow, they become large and pithy. Keep picking to keep the vine producing.

A member of the cucumber family, squash is easy to grow; in large containers with trellises so the plants can climb. Thin plants so you have three or four good stems going, and give squash good sunlight and lots of water. The plants are quite attractive and can be used as decoration for patio or terrace. Feed judiciously once plants are growing, and remember to pick early and often. Summer squash include

Early White Bush
Gold Nugget
Cocozelle
Summer Crookneck

Winter squash include

True Hubbard
Butternut

SWISS CHARD

This is an overlooked vegetable that is very tasty and extremely good for you. (There are many fine ways to prepare it.) One planting can be harvested for many months and often into late fall. Where spinach or lettuce might bolt, chard can, if necessary, tolerate hot weather. Chard can be grown in large bushel baskets or in the garden. It needs thinning, but they can be used for cooked greens. Leave about 2 to 4 inches between plants. There is no need for successive plantings because chard can be cut continuously and still produce new leaves.

These are virtually foolproof vegetables that can take almost untenable conditions and still produce a harvest, so do try chard. Good varieties include

Rhubarb Chard
Lucullus

TOMATOES

There are few things that beat the sweet luscious taste of freshly picked tomatoes. And tomatoes are perhaps the most popular of the vegetable crops to grow for the neophyte gardener. There are varieties specifically bred for container growing and resistant to diseases. You can start your own plants from seed, but many people I know buy prestarted seedlings because there is a good variety available.

Tomatoes need warm temperatures and as much sun as possible to produce a good crop. Set the pots on balconies, porches, or even an outdoor windowsill. Tomatoes are climbers and will need to be staked.

Give the plants plenty of water, and good feeding with a tomato-type food (sold at nurseries). Keep the plants growing continuously so you have a good harvest. Fertilize about a week after you transplant the seedlings and again in about 2 weeks. While plants are producing fruit fertilize every week.

Pollination of tomato blossoms is done by shaking the plant (presupposing there are no bees in the area). New blossoms open daily over a long period of time. Keep tomatoes at temperatures above 60°F. at night or they may not set fruit. Very warm temperatures, over 95°F., will affect them adversely too, so shelter plants from extreme sun on very hot days.

Thin tomato plants by removing the small suckers as they form. These are the tiny first two or three leaves that appear between the main stem and the foliage. Depending upon the variety, tomatoes should bear within 70 to 80 days after seed planting.

There are many varieties available, including
Gardener's Delight
Small Fry
Tiny Tim
Hybrid Patio
Spartan Red

FRUIT

Some years back when I bought a Bonanza Peach for container growing I was skeptical about these tiny trees that produce luscious fruit
(or so they were advertised). Today I know better—dwarf fruit trees
are excellent as container plants and do immensely well if given some
moderate care. You can grow peaches, nectarines, apricots, oranges,
limes, and lemons. Indeed, there is a veritable basket of bounty from
small fruit trees.

The delightful thing about fruit trees indoors is that they can, when
necessary, double as pot plants. Citrus are incredibly beautiful when
well grown, and the Bonanza Peach has often graced my plant room.
You can start citrus from seed of fruit purchased at groceries, but getting them to germinate may be difficult, so it is best to buy small trees
at nurseries. (There are many, many fine varieties.) And, you will be
assured of fruit. Home-grown varieties many times do not bloom, and
if they do, they may not set fruit.

Besides peaches, citrus, nectarines, and apples, you can now buy
seedlings of the more exotic fruits like figs and mangoes. Explore this

79

world; there is an incredible variety of plants and a fun experience in growing them.

Dwarf fruits are easy to grow and bear fruits as large as their standard-sized cousins. There are two types of dwarfs: natural, such as the Bonanza Peach, and the kumquat, or standard varieties, dwarfed by special techniques. They are grafted onto either growth-inhibiting root systems or seedling trees. Food accumulates in the upper part of the tree to produce more fruits. Roots do not receive as much food and thus do not grow extensively, so the tree is dwarfed, making it a suitable container subject in a tub or box.

There are, as mentioned, many varieties available, and the easiest to grow in and around the home are the Bonanza Peach and the citrus. You can certainly try others too if you have space. Trees are available at nurseries or from many mail-order suppliers.

STARTING WITH FRUIT TREES

It is fine to start some citrus seeds in soil and grow your own peaches or what have you, but if you want fruit-bearing trees, you will have to buy the dwarf varieties already in cans and growing well at nurseries. There is an incredibly good selection, and this is almost a surefire way of getting healthy, mature trees that will bear fruit.

If the tree is in a can, have the can cut at the nursery, and get the new plant immediately into a new container when you get home. Do not let it lie around and dry out because such treatment worsens the transplanting shock and the plant may never survive. If a fruit tree is in plastic, remove it from its container by tapping the edge of the pot on a table rim and letting the entire root ball fall into your hand. Have a new container with soil ready, and put the tree in place.

Fruit trees are a blessing for the nature-starved gardener in an apartment—a blessing in sight as well as taste—but they do have special requirements. Most need some sunlight during the day or they will not bloom to bear fruit. Ideally, a spot outside on a porch or balcony is what they want during the warm months. Most dwarf fruit trees will require a 10- or 14-inch pot, so be prepared, and do use a good rich potting soil. Prepare the tub by placing drain shards and a layer of

Put in pot shards for drainage

Fill ⅔ full with potting soil

Center tree in pot, spread roots

Fill in with soil, water thoroughly

How to Pot Dwarf Fruit Tree

Cut metal can

Carefully remove tree

Prepare new container;
drainage stones, potting soil

Planting; center tree, spread
out roots, firm soil and water

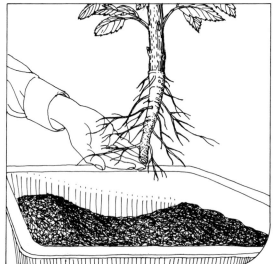

Removing Tree for Tub Planting

gravel in place. Now add some charcoal chips to keep the soil sweet (this soil must stay in the pot for several years). Put a mound of soil in place, and center the tree. If it is too low, add some soil to the mound; if it is too high, remove some soil. Fill in and around the tree with more soil, and firm down with your thumbs. Fill the container to within 1 inch of the top, and settle the soil by tamping it down with a blunt-edged stick. Watering is vital to fruit trees because they can consume great quantities of moisture and must have it to produce their yield. Water thoroughly; this means two or three times. Put the plant in a bright place that has good air circulation. Remember to get saucers for the tubs, to catch excess water, and also the movable dollies sold at nurseries so you can move trees around without trouble.

If your outdoor space is limited, you will have to be content with only a few varieties of peach and some citrus, and even these will take extra care to get them going their best. But, as mentioned, if you have that little outdoor area, including a doorway, you can grow many kinds of fruit.

Except for figs and mangoes, most fruit trees prefer a somewhat cool place during the day, say, 70°F., and 60°F. at night. Mist leaves frequently with fresh water to provide good humidity. Keep soil evenly moist, never dry, because dryness over even a short time can kill the tree. Deep soakings are recommended for fruit trees so all soil becomes really wet.

Routine care against insect invasion is a must. Scale is a common pest of fruit trees, and you must get rid of it when you see it. These insects look like small, hard, and oval brown shells attached to leaves and stems; a sticky-looking substance on leaves may also be an indication of scale. Use a soap and water mixture to eliminate the pests or a chemical such as rotenone.

Peach

Dwarf peach trees make handsome ornamental plants in and around the house. They rarely grow more than 4 feet tall, and fruits are large. Trees are at nurseries in early spring ready for planting and will need large tubs, say 12 to 16 inches in diameter. They require excellent watering and good sunlight to prosper, so keep the trees on a sunny porch or patio. Feed them regularly and protect them from insects, although it is rare for pests to bother a few trees.

Deciduous peach trees will lose their leaves in fall and be dormant until early spring. Plants need coolness at this time, but if it is extremely cold, they need protection. Mulch and cover the trees with cardboard to help keep them in good health. Give trees one good soaking before really cold weather arrives. Then find a sheltered outdoor

The Bonanza Peach is a well known dwarf with large fruit. It can be grown in tub or in the ground. (Photo courtesy Armstrong Nurseries)

spot for them, and give them only scanty watering until warm weather. When soil thaws and weather is warming, start watering again for a new season of harvest. Two good varieties are

Bonanza Dwarf
Stark Scarlet

Citrus

Dwarf citrus trees are now available in many varieties and make handsome trees for the home as well as produce. There are oranges, lemons, or limes to try, and each is worthwhile, although most people prefer the oranges.

Like most house plants, citrus trees enjoy the summer outdoors and will thrive in a protected sunny spot. See that they get plenty of water, and fertilize them every other watering, especially when they are bearing fruit. Keep trees sprayed with a fine mist of water to ward off insect attack and be alert for scale. If you see tiny, hard, and oval brown insects on plants, buy appropriate remedies. Here are a few of the dwarf citrus available

Calamondin Orange
Ponderosa Lemon
Persian Lime

STRAWBERRIES

I think everyone likes strawberries, and this is a simple crop for home harvesting. Pre-started plants, sold at nurseries, can be grown in planters, tubs, or the conventional strawberry jar. Plants need excellent drainage, so plant accordingly, with enough stones at the bottom of the tub to prevent excess water from standing. Give strawberries a warm sunny place—patio or backdoor area—and do water them copiously; they need plenty of moisture.

Plant strawberries at the proper depth, neither too deep nor too shallow. They should have soil to the crown of the plant, which divides the tops from the roots. When plants start growing, add some fertilizer. Pick off flowers that appear until July; plants should start to bear about a month later. Strawberries can also be grown effectively and successfully in hanging baskets. Almost any variety you find at nurseries is satisfactory.

PAPAYAS

Papaya in a pot? Why not? This is a delicious tropical fruit but you will have to start your own plants from seed. After you have eaten a papaya, wash the seeds well and try to remove the slick outer coating. Cover the seed with about ⅛ inch of soil in a container. Keep it in a warm bright place. Germination is tricky, so plant several seeds and do not be too disappointed if nothing happens. Seeds should start sprouting in about 4 to 8 weeks. If they do not, you have done something wrong, so try again.

Once plants are up they can be transplanted in individual pots. They will need copious water in summer but not as much in winter. Keep repotting plants every 6 months, and pray. These plants are strictly for the adventurous.

FIGS

Recently everbearing fig trees have been offered by mail-order suppliers. I have not tried them, but the idea of having a fig tree is appealing. I have, however, grown seedlings of fig trees (from my property) in large containers and can thus vouch for the plant. It is handsome and will bear fruit if you can give it ample sunlight, which means balcony or patio growing.

The trees never get too large, about 4 feet is maximum, and during the growing season (spring, summer) need plenty of water to thrive. In winter plants naturally rest, so reduce watering and store in a cool (but not freezing) area—perhaps an enclosed porch or garage.

Fresh figs, of course, are a delight to eat and rarely available at markets, so here is a case of really having something different and delicious at the same time. *Everbearing* is the most commonly available variety.

There are small citrus and standard-sized ones; all make fine plants and dwarfs are especially well suited to container growing. (Photo by author)

CANTALOUPES

Cantaloupes (muskmelons) are fun to grow. They grow fast, and on a trellis they climb and climb; kids get a big bang out of them. High heat is needed (about 80 to 90°F.) to start melon seeds. Lower night temperatures can start rot in plants. Making the transplant is somewhat difficult too because melon roots hate to be disturbed, so this is another crop for the adventurous. (Honeydew and Cranshaws are too tough to try.) Be sure to have manure or compost in the soil, and keep melons plenty moist. Too much rain or cold will produce bad melons. When the melons are ready for harvesting be sure they have buckets of water, but not so much during the ripening period. A long growing season is needed, about 80 to 90 days, depending upon variety. Buy disease-resistant varieties when possible. Minnesota Midget is the choice cantaloupe for beginning gardeners.

Melon ripening on the vine. (Photo by Barr)

WATERMELONS

Normally I would say forget watermelons because they require a lot
of space. However, recently delicious midget varieties called icebox
size have appeared on the market. Plants can be grown on fences or
in tubs if they have a support to grow on (half barrels are especially
good, using three or four plants to a tub). Plants mature in 75 to 85
days.

Melons require heat and more heat to grow really well, and they
need plenty of water to prosper; without it blossom-end rot occurs.
They will also need training, staking, and tying, so be ready to spend
some time on melons if you want them. The best varieties for tub or
planter growing are

New Hampshire Midget
Sugar Baby

HERBS

Herbs have more to offer than you think. They are essential for many tasty dishes; fresh herbs far excel the bottled ones you buy at stores; and you can use herbs to make scented things like sachets or just for fragrance in the kitchen. Growing herbs is not difficult, and even if you are an apartment dweller, there are many, many herbs you can grow at your windows for culinary dishes or fragrant teas or for scent: sweet basil, chives, chervil, tarragon, summery savory, rosemary, thyme, sage, sweet marjoram, fennel, parsley, and dill.

WHAT TO GROW HERBS IN

Like vegetables, herbs can be housed in a variety of containers: window boxes, barrels, homemade wooden containers, and clay pots. Make sure any container is at least 4 inches deep and 18 to 20 inches long, provide drainage holes, and be sure to have a saucer device or tray underneath to catch excess water. Most herbs need a good deal of water because a scanty watering will not produce good plants.

If you have shelves at the windows, and this is a good idea for herbs because they are basically small plants, you can grow dozens of herbs in pots and they will prosper from good light and sun. Vegetables and fruit trees need somewhat larger containers, but with herbs you can utilize almost any size of planter. Some herbs do grow very tall outdoors, such as dill, but indoors they adapt and will not grow as tall, and they can be pinched back when necessary. Most herbs will thrive in 4- or 5-inch pots with little trouble. No matter which container you select, be sure to allow enough space so herbs do not become crowded.

GROWING HERBS INDOORS

Use a good rich soil composed of 3 parts loam, 1 part sand, and 1 part compost. Be sure that all materials are thoroughly mixed. Put a layer of small stones or shards in the bottom of the container. Fill with soil, and then carefully transplant the tiny seedlings bought at nurseries into the soil. Dig small holes first; put plants in place with as much of the old root ball intact as possible. Firm the soil around the collar of the plants and tamp down to eliminate air pockets in the soil.

Thoroughly soak the soil, and set the plants in a bright sunny window. Tarragon and chervil will need some shade; other herbs can take full sun.

Herbs can tolerate more abuse than standard house plants, but avoid prolonged periods of extreme dryness or high temperatures. Keep a good circulation of air in the window area because few plants will thrive in a stagnant condition.

Keep herbs well watered (dryness *must* be avoided), and once a week soak pots in the sink so soil is really moist throughout. A great deal of successful herb growing depends upon good insect control. Avoid high temperatures, dry air, and a lack of fresh air because these conditions create a breeding place for red spider mites.

Fertilize with a soluble plant food once a month; keep plants well trimmed. You can use herbs fresh as they come off the plant, or dry and store them for future use. Some herbs are perennials: Once planted they come back year after year; annuals will only live one season and must be started again the following year.

Herbs are now available at many stores in kits with seeds, peat pots, and planting mix. Supposedly all you do is add water to start them growing. But as mentioned previously, this method is expensive and difficult, so stick to starting your herbs from seed.

HARVESTING AND DRYING

Herbs are a joy to use when they are fresh, but you can also preserve them. You can harvest and dry your own crops in one afternoon to give as gifts or use later as needed. Harvest (cut) herbs when they have the maximum amount of essential oils—when they are at their best, which is just when the buds come into flower.

Cut perennial herbs about two-thirds down the stalk; with annuals, leave a few inches for a possible second growth. Label and keep each herb separate because once herbs are dried they look very much the same. The drying process removes the moisture from the foliage. To dry plants, remove all yellowed leaves and coarse heavy ends. Rinse plants lightly. Take the fresh leaves from the stalk and put them on a screen; a house window screen is fine, or use any grill-type unit. The idea is to get a good circulation of air around the leaves. Set the screen in a dry and shady but well-ventilated area; an attic works fine. Turn the leaves a few times a day so air reaches all surfaces. The process should take three or four days.

Another way to dry herbs is to tie the leafy stems into bundles and hang them on cords in the attic. Still another way is to dry them in the oven, but it is difficult to regulate temperature, and too often the heat scorches the leaves and oils are evaporated. However, if you want to oven-dry herbs, put the leaves on a screen or baking sheet, and keep the oven at low heat (250°), with the door open. Feel leaves to see if they are dry.

Once herbs are dried (by any method), keep them in *labeled* glass jars. Watch them for a few days to make sure you have gotten all moisture out. If you see any moisture inside the jar, remove the leaves and dry them some more.

HERBS TO TRY

BASIL. This annual makes a good house plant, but do not let it bloom or set seed. Needs good moisture, sun, and moderate feeding. Watch out for red spider mites; if they attack, wash leaves with soapy water and rinse thoroughly. Easily started by seed in July or August.

BORAGE. Easily cultivated at a sunny window, this annual herb needs well-drained rich soil. Either sow a few seeds in fall or start young plants (from nurseries).

Dill is easy to grow and affords fine flavoring for recipes. (Photo by author)

Thyme is another excellent flavoring herb and grows well indoors and out.
(Photo by author)

CHIVES. A popular potted plant generally available at supermarkets. Keep in moist soil; snip as needed. Likes sun.

DILL. Sow a few seeds in a pot in late summer or early fall, and keep plant in bright light with lots of water. Cut as needed for seasoning.

PARSLEY. This favorite hardy biennial adds much to salads and cooked dishes. Seed is easily sown almost any time, and sunlight and coolness will provide good growth. (Soak seed 24 hours before sowing.) Likes good air circulation.

ROSEMARY. A perennial, rosemary needs a cool window with bright light. Likes a rich soil with excellent drainage. Does best in somewhat larger pots than most herbs.

SAGE. Another easily grown house plant, sage is excellent for seasonings. You can sow seeds almost any time. Give good sun and plenty of air with even moisture for a good harvest.

SWEET MARJORAM. An upright perennial that can be started from seed almost any time, or buy seedlings at nurseries in fall. Needs sunlight and good even moisture. Watch for insects; if any are found, wash thoroughly to eliminate them.

THYME. Thyme needs lots of sun to really prosper and likes coolness. Provide a well-drained soil. Even if you do not eat this herb it makes a pretty house plant.

WINTER SAVORY. Purchase young plants in autumn and grow at a bright window Needs well-drained soil and even moisture.

SUPPLIERS

Burgess Seed and Plant Co., Box 2000, Galesburg, Michigan 49053. 68 pages, 8½ x 11. Vegetables, 26 pages. Varieties specially selected for home gardeners. Many unusual items.

W. Atlee Burpee Co. (Free from your nearest Burpee branch): Philadelphia, Pennsylvania 19132. Clinton, Iowa 52732. Riverside, California 92502. 166 pages, 6 x 9.

Farmer Seed and Nursery Co., Faribault, Minnesota 55021. 84 pages, 8 x 10. Complete. Special attention to midget vegetables.

Henry Field Seed and Nursery Co., 407 Sycamore St., Shenandoah, Iowa 51601. 128 pages, 8½ x 11. A complete catalog. Wide variety selection. Many hard to find items.

Gurney Seed and Nursery Co., 1448 Page St., Yankton, South Dakota 57078. 64 pages, 15 x 20. Emphasis on short-season north country varieties.

Joseph Harris Co., Moreton Farm, Rochester, New York 14624. Box 432, Gresham, Oregon 97030. 84 pages, 8½ x 11. Vegetables, 39 pages.

J. W. Jung Seed Co., Station 8, Randolph, Wisconsin 53956. 70 pages, 9 x 12. Everything for the garden. Vegetables, 18 pages.

Earl May Seed and Nursery Co., 6032 Elm St., Shenandoah, Iowa 51601. 88 pages, 9½ x 12½. Wide choice of varieties.

Nichols Garden Nursery, 1190 No. Pacific Highway, Albany, Oregon 97321. 88 pages, 8½ x 11.

L. L. Olds Seed Co., 2901 Packers Ave., Box 1069, Madison, Wisconsin 53701. 80 pages, 8 x 10. Vegetables, 30 pages; carefully written guide to varieties.

Geo. W. Park Seed Co., Greenwood, South Carolina 29646. 116 pages, 8¼ x 11¼. A guide to quality and variety flowers and vegetables.

Seedway (formerly Robson Quality Seeds), Hall, New York 14463. 35 pages, 8½ x 11. Vegetables, 19 pages.

Harry E. Saier, Dimondale, Michigan 48821. 32 pages, 5½ x 9. Vegetables, 19 pages. General catalog 75¢. Ask for Vegetable catalog—it's free.

R. H. Shumway Seedsman, 62 Cedar St., Rockford, Illinois 61101. 92 pages, 10 x 13. Complete.

Stokes Seeds Co., Box 548 Main Post Office, Buffalo, New York 14240. 150 pages, 500 different vegetable and 800 different flower varieties.